# For Henry

Canada

FSC
www.fsc.org

MIX
Paper from
responsible sources
FSC® C102842

Robin Mitchell Cranfield

# Wings, Waves & Webs

## PATTERNS IN NATURE

GREYSTONE KIDS

GREYSTONE BOOKS • VANCOUVER/BERKELEY/LONDON

## Spotting Patterns

Anything repeated in a regular way can form a pattern.
A circular shape repeated again and again
becomes a dotty pattern that we call "spots."

What else can be arranged into a pattern?
Simple things like colors or numbers, and
there are even patterns to our days and our thoughts.

This book is about patterns we can see in nature:
some are big, some wild, some beautiful,
in rivers and snowflakes and eggshells and clouds.

Let's find patterns!

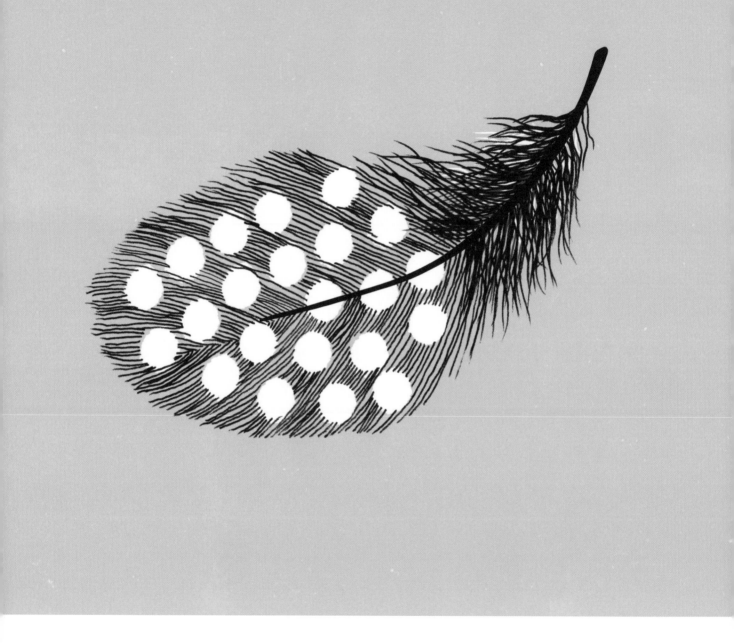

Spots

Some of these rounded marks are neat and orderly and some are freely sprinkled. This ladybug can be identified by its exact number of spots, while a guinea fowl can lose a feather with twenty-two spots and never even notice!

Stripes |||||

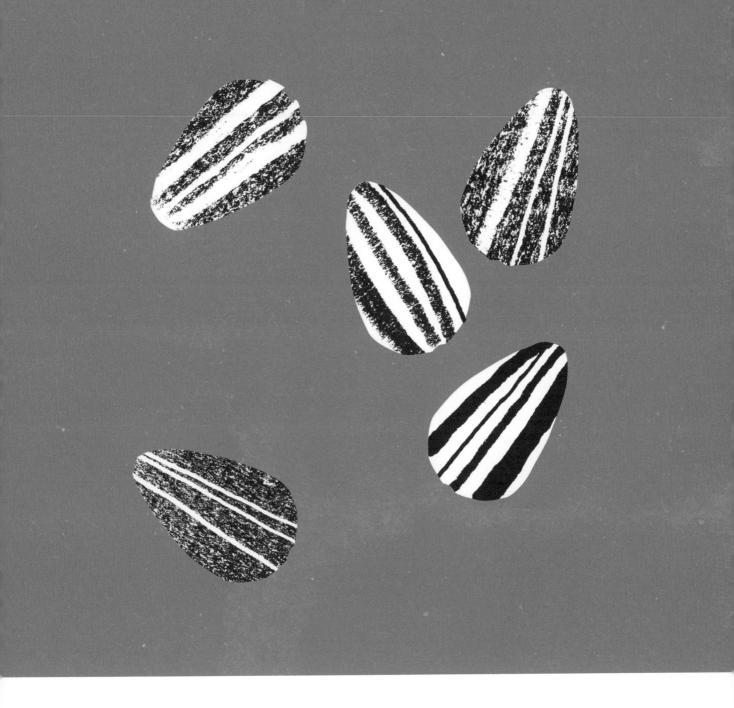

Bold patterns of lines dazzle the eye. A skunk's thick stripes warn predators,
"Stay away or you'll be sorry!" Sunflower seeds send a happier message:
"Time for a snack!"

Spirals

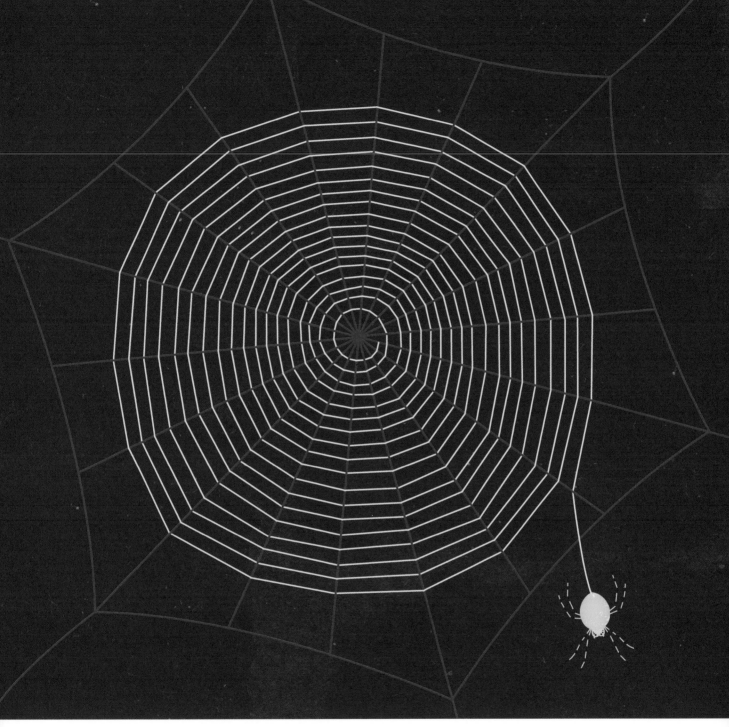

**golden orb weaver**

Spirals grow outwards round and round in ever-swirling circles. A spider's web gets bigger and bigger with every swirl. A snail's shell spirals in two directions, growing both wider and taller.

Mirror Symmetry

Mirror symmetry is balanced: each side is a reflection of the other. Balance helps creatures move, like how a butterfly's symmetrical wings help it float and fly through the air.

water lilies

Radial Symmetry ✳

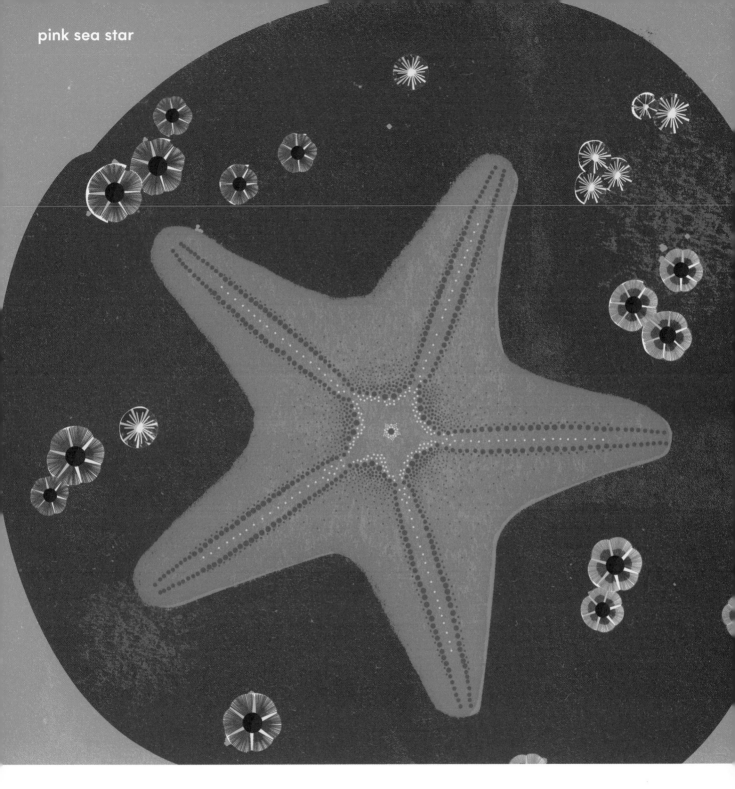

A starfish can walk in any direction. A lily welcomes passing dragonflies from every angle. How can they do this? Their petals and arms grow evenly around their middles, giving them radial symmetry.

ocean waves, seashore

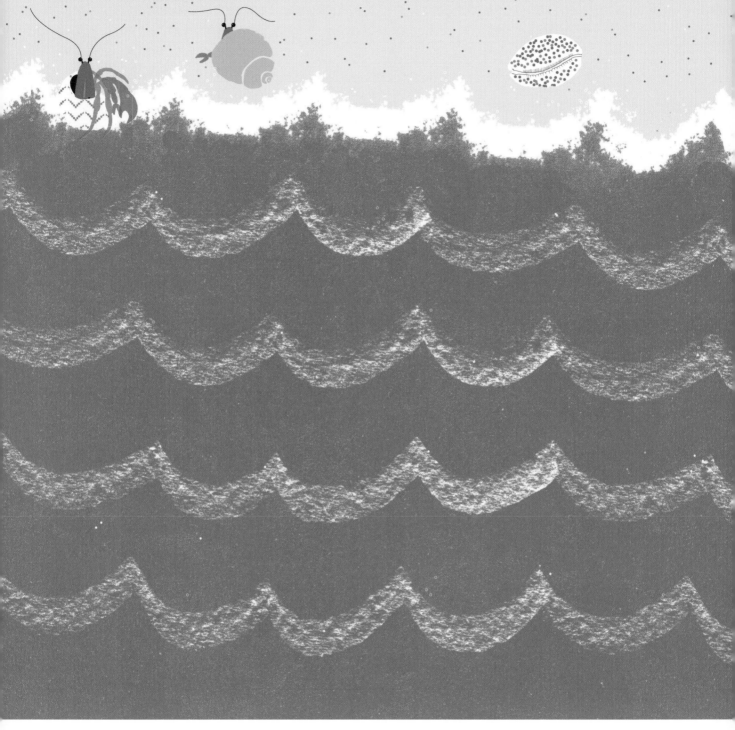

Waves

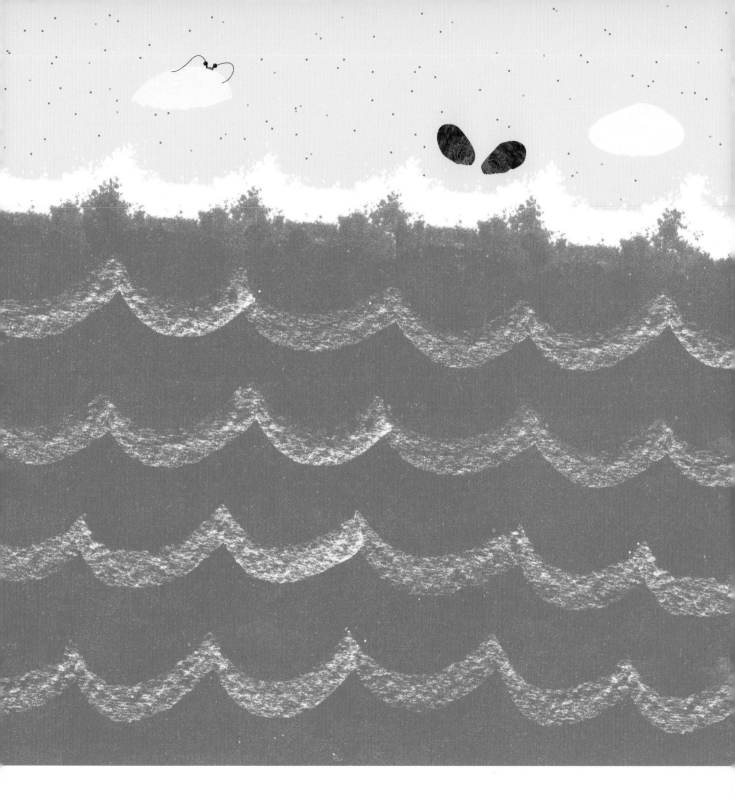

Waves travel forward, through time and space, rolling up and down.
Many waves, like sound and light, are invisible to us, but the white foamy
crests of ocean waves let us see this pattern of moving energy.

leopard tortoise

Honeycomb

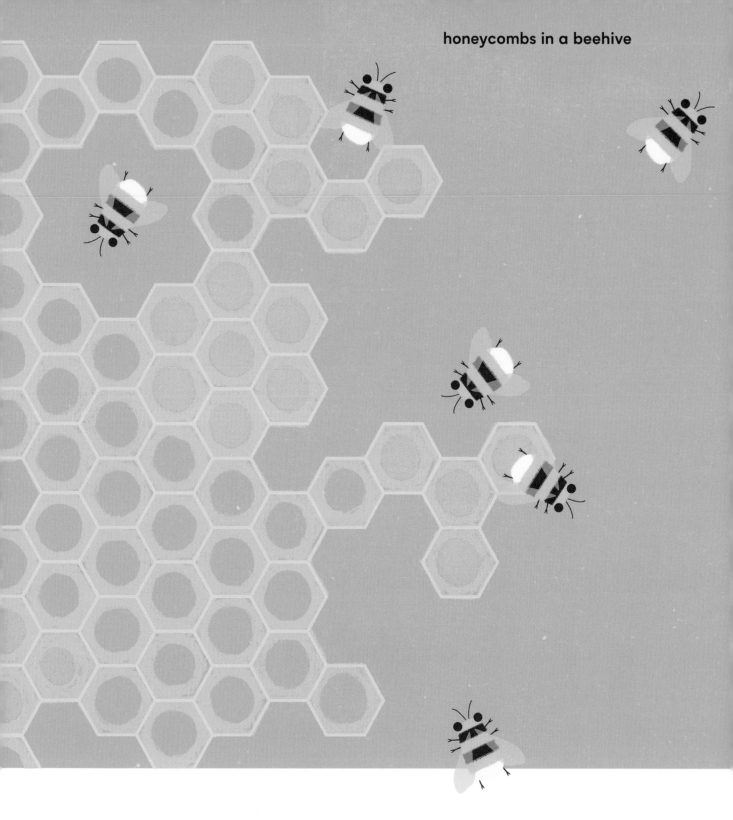

A hexagon shape has six sides. When these shapes are packed together they form a honeycomb pattern. Snugly tiled hexagons make safe and sturdy homes for tortoises and honeybees.

Cracks

Cracking is a wild pattern full of surprises. As a little chick grows, its eggshell can't stretch to keep up. Cracks appear and soon the chick does, too! Cracking often decorates dry surfaces, like the caps of these mushrooms.

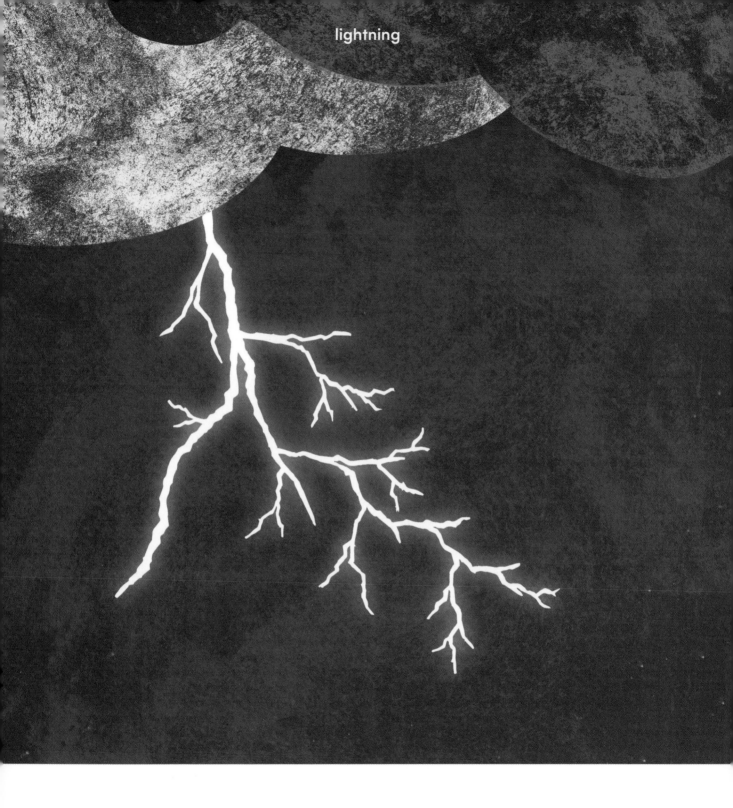

Branching

Branching patterns repeat the same or similar shapes over and over again in different sizes. Lightning branches as it fills the sky, while tiny ice crystals branch into delicate snowflakes as they grow.

Meanders

butter stripe corn snake

Meanders are repeated curves that can flow smoothly for a long time. Meandering calms a river's flow and describes the way a corn snake moves as it travels over the ground.

murmuration of starlings

Collective Motion

Fish travel in swift and graceful schools. Starlings fly in groups, too. Like fish or birds, when we join hands in a circle or jump up to dance to a tune, we form our own patterns of collective motion.

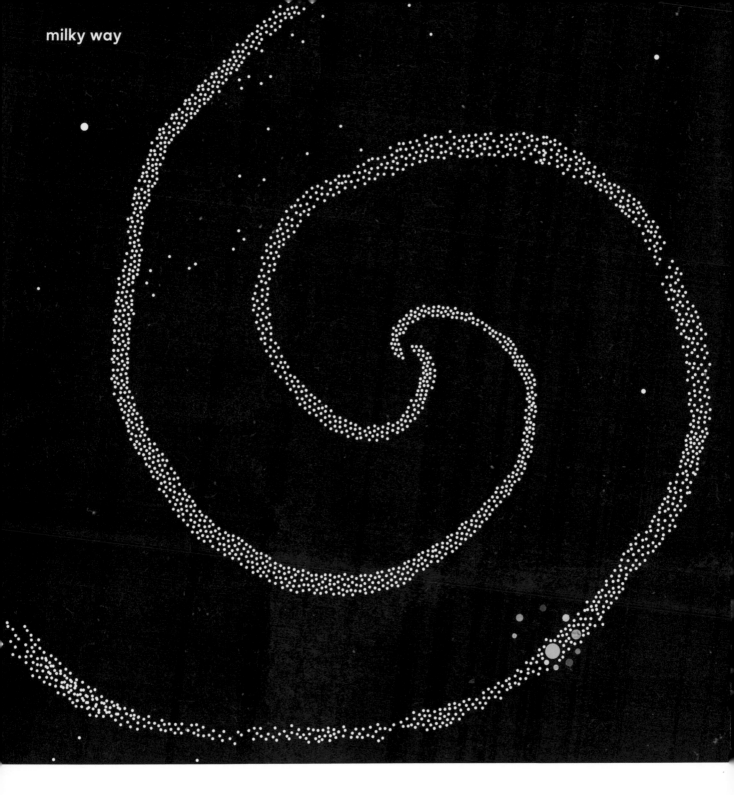

milky way

Spots, stripes, spirals, and so many more. Nature is full of patterns: inside, outside, up in the sky, on wings, waves, and webs. Wherever you go, you know what to look for!

**swallowtail butterfly**

Now . . .

which patterns can you find?